World Series Champions: Cleveland Guardians

Pitcher Corey Kluber

First baseman Jim Thome

WORLD SERIES CHAMPIONS

CLEVELAND GUARDIANS

JOE TISCHLER

CREATIVE EDUCATION / CREATIVE PAPERBACKS

Published by Creative Education and Creative Paperbacks
P.O. Box 227, Mankato, Minnesota 56002
Creative Education and Creative Paperbacks are imprints of
The Creative Company
www.thecreativecompany.us

Art Direction by Tom Morgan
Book production by Ciara Beitlich
Edited by Jill Kalz

Photographs by Alamy (Tribune Content Agency, UPI), AP
Images (Associated Press, Mark Duncan), Getty (Bettmann,
Jonathan Daniel, Diamond Images, Jason Miller, National
Baseball Hall of Fame Library, Photo File, Tom Pidgeon, Rich
Pilling, The Sporting News), Shutterstock (Sean Pavone),
Wikimedia Commons (Bain News Service)

Library of Congress Cataloging-in-Publication Data
Names: Tischler, Joe, author.
Title: Cleveland Guardians / Joe Tischler.
Description: Mankato, MN : Creative Education and Creative
    Paperbacks, [2024] | Series: Creative sports. World Series
    champions | Includes index. | Audience: Ages 7-10 | Audience:
    Grades 2-3 | Summary: "Elementary-level text and engaging
    sports photos highlight the Cleveland Guardians' MLB
    World Series wins and losses, plus sensational players
    associated with the professional baseball team such as José
    Ramírez."-- Provided by publisher.
Identifiers: LCCN 2023008179 (print) | LCCN 2023008180
    (ebook) | ISBN 9781640268210 (library binding) | ISBN
    9781682773710 (paperback) | ISBN 9781640009912 (pdf)
Subjects: LCSH: Cleveland Guardians (Baseball team)--
    History--Juvenile literature. | Cleveland Indians (Baseball
    team)--History--Juvenile literature. | World Series (Baseball)-
    -History--Juvenile literature.
Classification: LCC GV875.C7 T57 2024 (print) | LCC GV875.C7
    (ebook) | DDC 796.35709771/32--dc23/eng/20230306
LC record available at https://lccn.loc.gov/2023008179
LC ebook record available at https://lccn.loc.gov/2023008180

Printed in China

1948 World Series Champions

Outfielder Kenny Lofton

CONTENTS

Home of the Guardians

Cleveland, Ohio, sits along the shores of Lake Erie. It is home to the Rock and Roll Hall of Fame. It is also home to the Cleveland Guardians baseball team. The team plays at a **stadium** called Progressive Field.

The Guardians are a Major League Baseball (MLB) team. They play in the American League (AL) Central Division. Their main **rivals** are the Minnesota Twins and Chicago White Sox. All MLB teams try to win the World Series to become champions.

Second baseman Nap Lajoie

Naming the Guardians

The AL was formed in 1901. The Cleveland Blues were one of its first teams. The team has had many other nicknames. Two of them were Naps and Indians. The Indians nickname lasted more than 100 years. Prior to the 2022 season, the name changed to Guardians. It comes from a bridge near the team's home stadium. On the bridge are statues known as the "Guardians of traffic."

Outfielder Tris Speaker

Guardians History

The Guardians reached the World Series only 3 times in their first 90 years. Twice they won, in 1920 and 1948! Tris Speaker was a player and manager for the 1920 team. They beat the Brooklyn Robins in the World Series.

Pitchers Bob Lemon, Bob Feller, and Gene Bearden led the 1948 team. Infielders Lou Boudreau and Joe Gordon provided power with the bat. They beat the Boston Braves. That was the team's last World Series win.

Shortstop Lou Boudreau

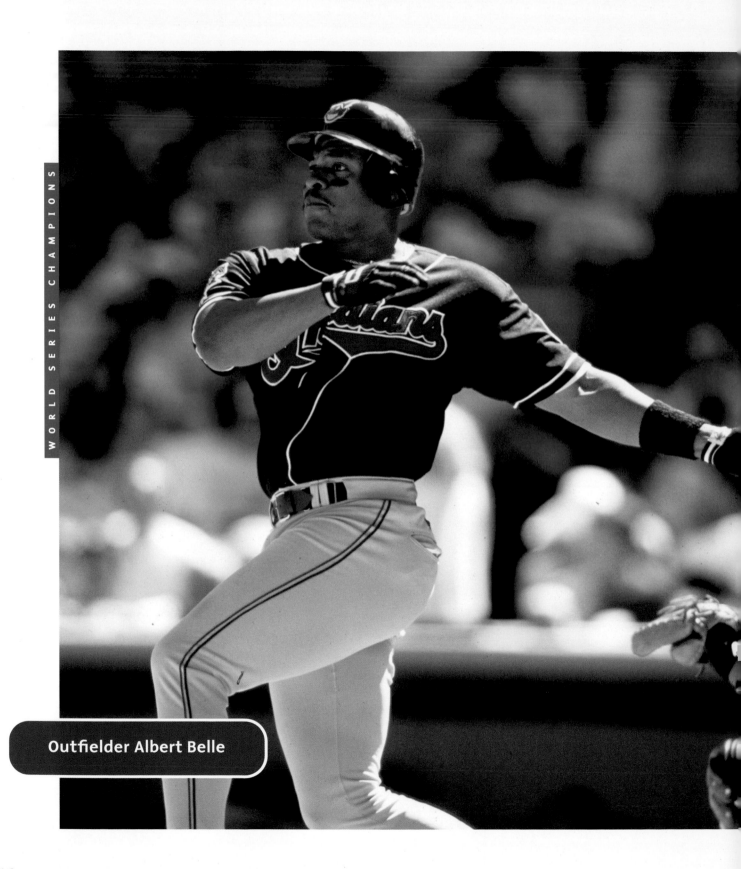

Outfielder Albert Belle

Power hitters Jim Thome and Albert Belle started a winning trend. In 1995, Cleveland made the **playoffs** for the first time in more than 40 years. The team won 100 games! They reached the World Series. But they fell to the Atlanta Braves. Cleveland returned to the World Series two years later. But they lost again.

Other Guardians Stars

The Guardians have continued their winning ways in the early 2000s. Starting pitcher Corey Kluber won two **Cy Young Awards**. Shane Bieber also won the award in 2020. Shortstop Francisco Lindor helped the team reach the 2016 World Series. He was great with his glove and his bat.

Pitcher Shane Bieber

Third baseman José Ramírez

All-Star infielders José Ramírez and Andrés Giménez helped Cleveland to a division **title** in 2022. Fans hope these stars can help bring Cleveland another World Series championship. They've been waiting for more than 70 years.

About the Guardians

Started playing: 1901

....

League/division: American
    League, Central Division

....

Team colors: navy blue and red

....

Home stadium: Progressive Field

....

WORLD SERIES CHAMPIONSHIPS:

    1920, 5 games to 2 over
    Brooklyn Robins

....

    1948, 4 games to 2 over
    Boston Braves

....

Cleveland Guardians website:
    www.mlb.com/guardians

....

Glossary

Cy Young Award—a yearly award given to the league's best pitcher

....

playoffs—games that the best teams play after a regular season to see who the champion will be

....

rival—a team that plays extra hard against another team

....

stadium—a building with tiers of seats for spectators

....

title—another word for championship

....

Second baseman Andrés Giménez

Index